Helianthus

In order to bloom, you must grow.

Heidi Gowthorpe

BookLeaf
Publishing

India | USA | UK

Helianthus © 2021 Heidi Gowthorpe

Presentation by *BookLeaf Publishing*

Web: www.bookleafpub.com

E-mail: info@bookleafpub.com

ISBN: 9789358361261

First edition 2021

To love. Rock bottoms. Adoration,

heartache, and the beauty that comes

through a pain so deep we have no choice

but to dig down and find our very roots.

Preface

Helianthus is a collection of poetry which evolved largely over the course of a year in which my life seemed to consist of repeatedly falling down and finding ways to get back up again.

I wrote this collection whilst trying to make sense of it all; both the beautiful and the painful sides of life. Each poem was written from a true moment of pain, despair, love, bliss, heartbreak, regret, loneliness or anger which seemed to soak me through. Writing this collection was catharsis, it became my way of letting it all out, and drying myself off.

I have tried to capture this period of my life in its rawest form, as I know I cannot be alone in many of my experiences through heartbreak, mental illness, addiction, healing and beginning to find my feet again, all within the chaos and loneliness of a worldwide pandemic and countrywide lockdown.

There have been moments within this period of my life where I have found hope, and magic within the deepest depths of despair. There have also been slithers of darkness in the places I thought were happiest. Those cracks within the spectrum, they are where the answers came through. In those moments of clarity the light flooded in and I found I was growing, heading towards the light. Just like a sunflower.

The name for this collection was a seed planted in my head by someone who very much gave me the encouragement I needed to write this book. Someone who once described me as "a Sunflower", and who's essence you will find running throughout many of these poems.

Helianthus; being the Latin name for Sunflower, is the joining of two words of Greek origin; "helios" meaning sun and "anthos" meaning flower. I chose the Latin name as a nod to the Greek Myth of Clytie and Apollo. This is the story from which the sunflower gains its meaning of loyalty, devotion and adoration. A story which I feel echoes some of the experiences I have shared within the pages of this book.

I hope you find yourself within these words. I hope they help you as they have helped me. And if you do (find yourself within them) then I hope you feel a little less alone.

"All flowers in time bend towards the sun"

~ Jeff Buckley

SUNFLOWER

As a new day creeps up on a new year of
living.

I close my eyes to the watching sky,

Inhale the sweet morning air.

And whisper a promise to my heart.

To find a home within myself.

To relax into my skin,

to my body,

to my being I surrender completely.

To stop fighting so hard against myself.

To accept the girl I have been and welcome
the woman I am becoming.

To let go.

To Forgive.

To pause.

To be patient.

To sit,

in stillness

and listen as the world moves and soars
around me.

To notice I am held by this earth and the
hands, arms and hearts of those who know
me.

To breathe more and think less.

To listen to the words of others

and the truth residing

deep within my gut.

To cherish those I am blessed to know,

and bookmark their holy space within my
chest.

To be more,

Honest.

To show myself grace.

To greet others with compassion.

To meet my own eyes across the fog of my
bathroom mirror.

To let a little more love in.

To lean into my heart when my head is
pulling away.

To stay rooted in the present, whenever I
find myself tripping forward.

To stay rooted,

when the desire comes to

start

running

backwards.

For the desire will come.

And when it does,

I promise to close my eyes and float on my
back through the ripples and the waves of
life.

To run the day loosely through my fingers.

To trust that I will stay afloat upon the tide.

I promise to notice the beautiful things.

To open my heart and bathe in the sunlight.
To hold my hands out to feel the rain.

Upon my skin.

BIG GOD

When I was young, I had no centre.

I was limbs,

Wild and flying everywhere.

All peripheries.

A hollowness at my centre like the shiny
tempered innards of an unwrapped kinder
egg.

I rattled when walking.

My heart, lungs, liver, and intestine; my
entrails just crashing around cacophonous
symbols inside my smallness.

Yet my edges softened when I ate.

I softened when I ate.

Inside and out.

Thoughts and flesh melted simultaneously
like ice cream down the side of a thick
thatched cone.

I slammed handfuls of sugar through my
lips.

Crammed it like a letter through a post box.

Listened as it fell down and down landing
in my swelling stomach with a thud.

Drowning out the sound of my thoughts
growing louder, and more violent with each
day I grew.

Expanded.

Stretched.

The more I fed the hollow inside me the bigger it seemed to swell until I was standing on the precipice of myself ready to jump.

I am sick, I am sore, I have hit the rock face first.

I needed a big god to fill my sweet centre.

I needed big hands to lift me down from my high horse.

I am hot and cold.

Slacklining the thin line between

self-righteousness and self-repulsion.

All I know is;

 I am empty.

So desperately hollow.

I need a big god to fill my sour centre.

I need big hands to lift me down from my

Trojan horse.

ANGEL

You said . . .

 I knew your eyes before I met you.

I had seen them in lucid, crackling dreams.

Somewhere in the cavernous, well of empty,

in the junk drawer of my brain.

Buried beneath hoarded feelings, old habits,

tired excuses.

Amongst the clutter of half-forgotten faces,

half remembered grudges, the blurred

edges of a childhood before memory's

begin.

There they were.

Yours.

I must have been waiting for them.

All this time.

To fix their gaze with mine,

To welcome them home.

FISHHOOK

When I saw you Lately, my heavy heart did overflow.

It swelled up to meet my rib cage, and it screamed to be let go.

In reply I felt a tiny pin prick,

as a silver fishhook shining,

Punctured chest, swelling lung, and brittle bone.

It came to find its resting place in warm metallic red,

on the left side of my breast, in my heart and Spinning head.

There it wound its wire so tightly, that it
stole away my breath.

Left me gasping in the moonlight for sweet
poetic bliss of death.

For a time it made a nest there, As my moth
like heart it beat for air.

A fluttering suffocation, caressing; planted
there with care.

Overnight it tightened with a strangling
grip, as side by side we slept.

Till one morning, with a tender tug.

A coaxing gentle kiss.

It hooked itself a heartbeat from its hollow

place of rest,

and my heart, it found a new home beneath

your warm and beating chest.

PISSING IN A RIVER

It's Raining again.

The sky is pissing rivers into the humble
dark night.

So soothing a sound, strange yet familiar.

Uneven yet constant.

Rising and falling like the breath within my
chest.

It lulls me to sleep.

Into waiting, heady, restless dreams.

Only to be woken, nestled in the small
tender hours, as it raises its voice, makes a

further argument for the case of staying
awake.

So sleep evades me again.

Slips from my grasp, like a scaled silver fish,

Washed away by the rain, the river swelling
above me.

 I lay in the darkness,

Between warm foreign sheets,

Listening. Serenaded by an aria of sky.

Feeling the patter of cool rain on my skin,
as if I lay on my back on the cold lead tiles
of the terrace roof, exposed to stars.

Baptised by the sky.

As the night ambles on to meet morning,

It subsides a little,

Driven west by a low rumbling gale,

A hollow whistle.

A yawn of wind through col-de-sacked
houses.

A route to empty nowhere.

A clatter with a tripping gate.

The ebbing trickle of the rain washes away
my lonely thoughts.

Rinsing out my skull like a salad spinner,

Swishing and swirling around,

A spin cycle.

Till I am calm and sombre.

Sober and Sad,

And blue as the rain for want of you.

ADDICTED

Darling, I've been thinking about your drinking.

Maybe we should talk.

Hold me tighter, than your lighter, else I'll flicker in the dark.

Put me in your pipe and smoke me too. I could be your cancer darling.

But, don't forget me, when you're sober Tuesday night.

When you're intoxicated, I'll be the one who waited, and held your hand until daylight.

Several whisky's later I could be your
radiator,

Put down Jack Daniels, I could be your
man.

I don't know how to leave you, but if I stay,
I don't think I'll make it through.

Just don't forget me, when you're sober
Tuesday night.

Honey your fixation, for this inhalation, it
won't draw me into you.

Though you're hallucinating, I'll be the one
who's waiting, I'm tired of tripping over
you.

You're hooked on fire water, I really think
we ought to prize the monkey from your
back.

So you, don't forget me, when you're sober
Tuesday night.

POACHED

The eggs bubbled over on the stove,

forgotten.

Coating the oven in a thin white foaming

film.

The pan boiling dry and black.

The acrid stench of burning worked its way

in smoky tendrils up my nostrils.

Burning.

Words spilled out of us both,

Spitting.

As though we were squeezed from our feet

like an old tube of toothpaste.

Rolling up and out of us on a hurricane.

Crusting crisp and white on our lips before
we could make sense of one another.

Holly silence abandoned in the space
between us, as we spat our pain into one
another like hot oil.

Eggs charcoaled and forgotten in a
desperate thirst of crude raw feeling.

The only semblance of a sunlit morning left
to bubble dry upon the stove.

ECHO

We are unravelling.

Standing side by side,

Amongst the silence.

Magnetised to the kitchen sink, watching
the world pass us by beyond the window.

She washes and I dry.

Side by side. Two women.

Both fraying at the edges as invisible
strings pull at the threads of us.

We Kaleidoscopically unravel in perfect,
beautiful, divine synchronicity.

An act of nature, to behold.

Unbeknownst to all around us.

This woman. Older than I. A mother. She
mirrors me so elegantly, so exactly, it
frightens the bones of me.

She folds and I feel I hold the weight of her
in my arms. Bone and flesh and sinew all
that's left, keeping her together.

I see the glass behind her eyes is cracking.

Just

like

mine.

Everything I had hidden is there, clear as day, staring straight back at me through honey irises.

Just

like

yours, I think.

Fragile as a round bubble floating in the washing up water,

Maybe one of us will burst.

Pop.

I wonder if she sees the thread of me reeling, running away from myself, in parallel.

In pathetic tandem with that of hers.

Nothing to do but watch it go.

Grasp at the last thread through open
fingers.

Hopeless, hapless, helpless.

 And so.

We unravel.

Stretched out thin and gapping, a
fisherman's jumper, sodden with dish water.

Two by two.

She and I.

She washes and I dry.

Side by side. Two women.

We find ourselves brought together by the same undoing.

Trying to twist ourselves in tangled spiderwebbed together.

Clinging on for dear life.

FAULT MODE

I am always chewing.

Chewing gum and cheek and tongue,

Till I'm sore and stiff of jaw.

Aching tension, tooth, and nail.

Teeth drill and push and pull.

Chewing up my thoughts till they're red
and bloody – raw.

Over thinking.

Over feeling.

Over feeding.

Over filling.

Cramming and stuffing.

Till I cannot.

feel

another

thing.

HOLY NET OF COMPULSIONS

 My mind is holy net of compulsions.

Every morning at 7.40 I Checked my body for underwear and excess fat before I stepped onto the school bus, haunted by

"that dream".

I checked the lock on the door 4 times before I was satisfied to leave it.

Yet It still held a small crook in my thoughts all day long.

My alarm was never to be trusted. My thoughts never to be trusted. My flesh - never to be trusted.

I checked my body 20 times today with cold hands,

Each time it seemed to fill me up with more hot revulsion.

I checked it again.

I said "cherry" over and over beneath every ladder just like an old friend told me.

It took me 10 years to shrug it off.

Now I just cross the road.

Avoidant.

I guess nothing's changed.

I Saluted magpies like my grandmother.

I craved so I ate.

I felt so I ate.

I cried rivers into my cereal bowl.

So I stopped.

I hugged the edge of my toilet bowl for lack
of a lover.

Sacrificed my teeth, my stomach lining, my
grip on reality to make a girl who fit.

Fit between cracks so no one could see her.

Fit into jeans made for children. Fit.

Fit better into the tiny space left for her in

the jigsaw puzzle.

But still I stuck out.

What kind of monster am I?

THAWING

 Beaten down by winds and woe,

Cherry blossom does but grow.

There's a manic beauty as the buds begin to
sow,

Love is blooming,

Love is aching,

Bursting through the snow.

MORNING NEWS

Today I could not be saited.

Not by any number of tricks.

Not by food, or sex, or mindless rabid
daytime TV.

The internal quiet was amiss, disturbed,
unbalanced, quite without warning.

By something foreign and unfamiliar,

Unhinging me from within.

Thoughts tangled beyond reason,

And I found I had to swallow you whole.

TERRACE; No 48

My little house sits empty,

Empty of anything worthwhile being filled
with.

There are wooden chairs. Four. A table and
a bed bound by sheets. Coffee cups piled
high in a scummy, silver, sink. Half-eaten
tins of beans, a half-finished novella
hugging the arm of a two-seater settee.

There are things. Materials, possessions.
My little house is brimming with them.

Full.

Yet empty of all else.

Like a film set after dark. Its falseness
glaringly apparent in the silver glow of

moonlight creeping in through a gap in the curtains.

Feelings have flown south for the winter.

Home degraded and demoted to a house.
Stripped of its former title. Shamed.

For all to see.

I sit astride the quiet.

Eyes squinting in the darkness of a bedroom.

The bulb nestled in the peeling light fixture above me died; I don't remember when.

I haven't the heart left to change it.

Your fingers put it there,

where I couldn't reach.

The last time.

Perhaps that's why mourning dress is black?

Now my world is like the ceiling light spluttered out and failed to give glow.

My world is without light.

I sit like a fattening buddha, lotus like in month old sheets. I allow the thought to drift upon me, wrap it around me like a shroud.

"What a year my heart has had".

I rub my chest as if I could thaw it, like hands desperate for gloves.

Sorry.

I whisper.

The letters crackle in the quiet, my voice breaks for lack of use.

The sound hangs in the air before the walls soak it up. Drink it in.

Sorry.

I whisper. To my heart.

I would imagine this is what loneliness must look like.

I mull it over whilst the kettle whistles on
the hob downstairs.

As it screeches to a halt.

A Dead stop.

 The silence resumes. But for the traffic
hum outside.

I imagine this is what loneliness must look
like.

OBSESSIVE COMPULSIVE DAUGHTER

Getting well is hell.

A self-proscribed minefield.

You take a step, close your eyes, take a breath, pray you'll make it. Hope the fallout isn't so bad. Cross your heart, hope nobody dies. Speak the words you've only ever said in silence. Take another step. Close your eyes. Pray you'll make it.

Hold your feet steady as the world crumbles around you.

Close your eyes. Call the doctor, ask for help. Tell the world you're broken, defected.

Have been ever since.

Read the book. Tell the truth. Read the book. Tell the truth. Close your eyes. Take a step. Spill the words all over the dinner table.

Words that you can never erase.

Close your eyes. Take a breath.

Watch them sit there. See the damage spread like the red wine stain on the cream sofa.

Numb the pain, Numb the pain, Numb the pain. Start again. Close your eyes. Take a breath. Tell the truth. Read the book.

I read it through three times before I was satisfied to say I'd read it. I wanted to digest

the words in full pages. Run them through
my head like rivers, as they unravel within
me. As I was drip,

drip,

drip

fed page upon page of courier font undiluted
truth. As I saw myself finally in printed
letters.

And so I folded in upon myself.

Origami paper thin.

I guess I'm just not ready.

YOUR POEM No. 4876

Today I miss you like a thunderstorm.

It pumps through my veins,

Like rabid poison.

The flutter that still rises up in my chest at

the thought of you.

Morse code for –

I

Still

Love

You.

I miss you holding me.

The way you could hold my whole self in

the fold of your arms.

A baby bird cupped between solid hands.

The radiating heat of you bleeding into me.

The warm unwashed scent of your hair on
my pillow, that lingered days after you had
gone.
 I miss.
I miss knowing the end of your joke, before
you've finished forming the words.
I miss the husk and depth of your voice.
The southern English vowels draped in
lazy Californian lilt.

I miss.
The pressure of your body on mine.
The hunger of your grip.

I miss knowing the glaze that swims over
your honey eyes when you are lost.

I miss the sound of your laughter. How it
burst from you untamed.

I miss the crease that formed in the corner of your bitten lips in the moments before a smile escaped them. As if it was caught there, undecided.

I miss.
I miss how soundly I slept on your chest. How I fell into the depths of sleep the moment my hair landed there. Soothed by the lullaby of your breath.

I miss long lazy mornings propped up on pillows sharing our dreams.

I miss.
I miss knowing I belonged.
Knowing you were home.
Knowing I was somebody to someone.

I miss the days when I didn't have to screw

the lid of myself so damn tight.

A deft twist with both hands.

To stop myself from spilling out.

Calling out.

A text.

A voicemail.

A letter sent with a stamp of tears and

sealed with a desperate kiss.

Some sort of yearning SCREAM across a

blank screen.

The resting water in my gut tells me I must

wait.

It takes time,

to heal a heartbeat.

To detangle oneself from another soul.

I must give it time.

Give it time.

Wait until it's time.

To come back home to you.

RENEW

In the mellow water I am baptised each evening.

In the dimming light I shrug off layers of myself as I peel my shirt from my shoulders, lower my body into the cup, naked and shining.

My skin submerging beneath the rippling crystalline surface, becomes Pink and white.

Marshmallow pigmented.

Blood at once races to the surface, kissing the underneath of my skin as it softens and plumps.

My body gives in, yields to the warmth.
Moses, cradled by the waiting water.

I sink deeper into the blue, submitting,
allowing myself to be swallowed whole.

Holding a beating breath behind pursed
lips.

I prize open my eyes beneath the wavering
surface and gaze through clear cut glass at
the yellow of the fluorescent bathroom light
swimming above me.

A window to the waiting world.

Lying there I Imagine I am blessed by the
orb floating above like a brilliant new moon.

I am baptised by Mother Earth in the tears
of her making.

Hovering encased beneath the surface, till
the beating in my chest begins to swell and
tighten to a thunderstorm.

Till the breath that resided between my
lungs runs dry.

I am hollowed out from within.

A pearlescent shell ready to renew.

I break the surface searching for air.

Desperately reborn into myself.

Washed of all else.

Purged of yesterday.

I pray for renewal.

POWDER BLUE SKY

Fly the nest little bird.

Launch yourself with fierce abandon into
the powder blue sky.

Shed your fears like moulting feathers.

Announce your starving mourning cry.

In secret I watch your maiden flight.

Through eyes laden with broken sleep.

Watch your zig zagged path across the
infinite blue.

You carve through cotton candy clouds.

You bless the world anew.

In slow motion dawn arises.

Chasing your tail with the richest pink.

Until at last the waking sun lights the
waiting sky ablaze.

Sends your shadow running wide.

Across the shimmered summer haze.

Little bird brought home upon a breeze.

Comes to rest upon my window ledge.

We observe a stain glass stalemate.

My own reflection in your marbled eyes.

Then off and up you fly.

And I,

Rooted to the spot.

Watch with a longing, lingering.

As you leave without goodbye.

ARETHA

Eye's drift closed.

As I float.

Socked feet gliding noughts and crosses
across the faded linoleum floor.

I lose track of myself as I fold and crash
into the embrace of Aretha Franklin's
sonorous voice.

It brims, spilling over the record player.

Fills me up in the way of something cool
and fizzing.

Running the length of my spine,

up and down again.

Vibrating right into the core of my solar plexus.

Humming like a quivering arrow straight into my heart.

"Ain't no way".

"Ain't no way"

With every running line puppet like my libs abandon me.

Drifting up and around me.

As the world plays out in full, magnificent colour, flickering behind closed eyes.

On their own, my feet wind and weave and sweep across the kitchen floor kicking up a dust bowl amongst the breakfast toast crumbs.

It hangs, suspended, caught between afternoon sun streams that trail in through the half open window.

It swirls around me as I spin, spinning in tandem with the record on the player.

I spin and she sings.

I am lost to her lullaby.

Yet in losing myself I feel,

So.

Very.

Free.

TANGERINE

I love these sweet spring mornings.

Alone, bathing in nature's quiet serenity.

The lull of a lazy half hour before the house
arises.

Before the walls fill with the hum of daily
life.

I sit in the sweet spot: the brick step poised
between the wild flowers.

Forget me nots sprouting up uninvited,
through the cracks between my feet.

The bitterness of tangerines on my tongue.

My hair ripples side to side sweeping my
shoulders in warm soft breezes.

Bird song washes over me, cascading and
tripping like a waterfall upon my ear.

I bask in the low slung yellow of a waking
sun.

A cat arching its back, feeling the warmth
of its caress upon my face.

A morning kiss, a breath of fresh air,
another sweet spring morning.

EPILOGUE IN BLOOM

I forgot I had roots.

Unwinding unwittingly below the dirt.

Whilst my petals have been wilting in harsh
sunlight and battering salty, sea roak gales,
my roots have held me steady.

Stayed proud and thick and true.

Deeply buried below soil and sorrow and
sinew in the dark and dust.

Now Autumn once more has come again.

And frosted loneliness makes cold my bed.

The soil set.

Rock solid.

Hard and harsh and full of cooling
whipping, knuckle white shame.

But.

Yet.

A small something in the crisp October air
this very morning.

The hushed whisper caught up upon a
breeze.

Reminds me I have roots,

How I had forgotten them.

Despite myself they are still spreading like young loves reaching fingers, clinging on bitterly below the earth.

Holding me steadfast and strong, eternally unyielding until I am ready to begin again.

Grounding me to the earth. Reminding me.

Spring will come again.

May will see me bloom.

I will unfold into the sweet kiss of sunshine once more.

All is not lost petal.

All is just waiting for the notion

to bloom.

www.ingramcontent.com/pod-product-compliance
Lightning Source LLC
Chambersburg PA
CBHW070918160726
48004CB00003B/1414